Contents

NEEDLE FELTING GUIDE

INTRODUCTION

Felt is the oldest textile known, and its history is fascinating. It is a non-woven fabric that pre-dates the spinning of fibers and weaving of cloth. It has been made by the nomadic tribe's of Central Asia for thousands of years.

These nomads herded sheep, goats, camels, and horses, and therefore had a ready supply of wool and hair with which to make felt. It was used to cover shelters and for making headdresses, bags, and clothing.

There is evidence of felt being made in Britain in Roman times. Traditional feltmaking continues in countries throughout the world, including Turkey, Afghanistan, and India, where feltmakers all have their own way of working. I have had the privilege of travelling to Kyrgyzstan where there is still a living culture of feltmaking.

My method is a variation on the rolling methods used by many people in the Middle East and Central Asia, both past and present.

Needle felting is a craft that involves repeatedly stabbing a needle into a piece of wool in order to stiffen and shape it into the desired form. It is becoming a popular method for creating small animal figures since the texture of the felted creations resembles an animal's fur. Other popular items that felters enjoy creating include foods, plants, and cartoon characters.

A special type of needle is used to manipulate the fibers by repeatedly poking itself into the ball of wool. The tip of the needle features small barbed notches that allow the fibers of the wool to be moved towards the center of the shape without being pulled back out when the needle is pulled out. The more this is done, the more rigid your shape will become.

Needle felting is also starting to become a popular form of stress relief, as the repeated motions of the needle can be very therapeutic. The best thing about needle felting is that you don't need much to get started!

What is the Difference Between Needle Felting and Wet Felting?

Needle felting, also known as dry felting, does not require the use of water to create the desired results. The result of dry felting is usually a three-dimensional object.

Wet felting involves the combining of wool fibers to create a piece of fabric by using water and soap. It can also be used to create two-dimensional artwork. Compared to other methods of textile creations, wet felting is a simple technique with multiple steps involving heat, moisture, pressure, agitation and a change in pH levels.

Nuno felting is a third technique invented in the 1990s by Australian artist Polly Stirling. Wool is incorporated into an open weave fabric like silk chiffon to create a lightweight felt. The term "nuno" actually lends itself from the Japanese term meaning "cloth."

Where Did Needle Felting Originate?

The History of Needle Felting

Felting, or the process of matting or interlocking wool fibers, is one of the earliest forms of textile creations. Unlike other methods, it does not involve any weaving or spinning to create fabric out of wool. It only consists of the matting or condensing of the fibers to result in a stiff creation.

The exact history of this craft is complicated to track down due to its long-standing history. Its origin has been featured in the stories of many different cultures including Sumerian and Greek legends. In the 1st-3rd century Greece, it was claimed that Saint Clement and Saint Christopher discovered felting when they had packed their sandals with wool to help minimize blisters while escaping persecution. At the end of their travels, they found that the wool had matted into felt possibly due to the moisture and movement that had occurred.

Needle Felting in Modern Times

This craft has been steadily rising in popularity over the past couple of decades. More recently, needle felted creations are a favorite among hobbyists who enjoy creating miniatures or "kawaii" figures. It is also starting to rival the popularity of coloring books due to its therapeutic nature and the simplicity of the activity.

What Supplies Do I For Needle Felting?

This craft actually doesn't require many supplies to get started! All you need is a needle, some wool and a piece of foam.

Needle Felting Needles

AAs previously mentioned, needle felting requires a specialized type of needle with notched tips. These tips allow the fibers to be pulled into the center of the wool to create a stiff felt. The more you poke with a needle, the stiffer the fibers will become.

Only small rapid movement's are required with the needle. You don't need to fully insert it into the wool to agitate the fibers. To avoid breaking the needle, it's also essential to remove the needle at the same angle that it was initially inserted. If the wool feels too stiff to insert a needle, don't force it! Use a smaller gauge needle to finish or move to a new area.

TYPES OF FELTING NEEDLES

There are four different types of felting needles: spiral, triangular, round, and reverse felting. These are primarily based on the cross-section shape of the needle but have other characteristics that differentiate them from each other.

Spiral, triangular, and reverse felting needles are actually all triangular in shape. The spiral needle features a twisted blade while the reverse felting has opposite notches that pull the fibers out of the shaped wool.

The reverse felting tool can be used as a finishing tool to manipulate the resulting texture or pull out an underlying color if needed. I wouldn't necessarily recommend it if you are just getting started, but it may be helpful if you decide to pursue this hobby further.

NEEDLE GAUGES

Felting needles are available in 32, 36, 38, 40 and 42 gauges. The higher the number, the thinner the needle. Use thicker needles for coarse wool and smaller gauges for thinner fibers. You can also use a smaller gauged needle when the wool becomes too thick.

It may be difficult to tell the size of your needle if you have multiple ones so take time to color-code them if needed. I would suggest using nail polish or a small strip of colored washi tape at the handle.

FELTING NEEDLE PENS

Pens (like this one here) can also help to improve your process. This pen can actually hold multiple needles at once (up to 3) so that felting is more efficient. It also has a more substantial grip attached that makes it easier to handle. There are a variety of tools out there to help with common needle felting issues. Experiment with different ones as you dive deeper into this craft.

WHAT IS THE BEST NEEDLE FOR NEEDLE FELTING?

Ideally, you should have multiple types of needles in a variety of gauges. Many kits may also include more than one needle. You can also purchase packs of needles at a pretty affordable price as you probably will end up breaking some anyway. If that's not an option, purchasing a 38-gauge needle would be a great choice as a beginner. The type of needle can vary based on your personal preference but selecting a spiral or triangular one would be best for getting started.

Needles also come with a varying amount of notches. A higher number of grooves would allow you to felt more efficiently but may not be necessary when trying to complete more detailed work. Keep that in mind while purchasing your needles.

Needle Felting Wool

There are numerous types of fibers you can choose from for your creations. You can use animal, plant and synthetic fibers for this craft but most felters use wool from a sheep. Different types of sheep can produce wool with varying characteristics so you may need to experiment with multiple types to find the one you like best. These may include Corriedale, Merino, New Zealand, Norwegian Lincoln, Romney, Drysdale, and many others.

Wool is usually graded in microns where the higher the micron correlates to the coarseness of the fibers. Not only is the roughness of the fiber a factor in selecting your wool, but the method on how the wool is processed can also affect your choice.

Wool Roving vs Wool Batts

Wool is available in two primary styles: roving and batts. Roving is wool that has been brushed with special padding (also known as being carded) until the fibers are all running in the same direction. It's best used for spinning. Batts are sheets of thick wool that have not been fully carded and consequently have kinks of fibers running in a variety of directions.

Both wool roving and batts are acceptable for needle felting as you will be using the needle to manipulate the fiber kinks anyway. However, batts may be easier to use since the fibers are already running wild in different directions.

Best Wool for Needle Felting

Not all wool will work well for needle felting. Some are great for wet felting (like Merino wool) but may not the best for the purposes of this craft. Fine wool will result in a softer, silkier texture but coarser wool is actually better for needle felting as the notches on the needle will grab on to the scales on the fiber easier. This will allow you to manipulate the wool much more efficiently.

For needle felting, you'll want to target a medium-coarse fiber. You want wool that is easy for the needle to hold on to but still has a smooth finish.

For beginners, you probably only need one color of the wool to get started. If you are anything like me, that's not going to cut it. When I get excited about a new creative hobby, I want options. I want colors.

This kit actually comes with 36 different colors of 3-gram packs of Merino wool. Some prefer Merino wool for wet felting, but the set actually works well for needle felting!

Merino wool (fine-medium) – Can be used for both wet felting and needle felting

New Zealand wool (medium-coarse) – Great for needle felting, less smooth finish vs Merino

Icelandic wool (coarse, hairy) – Thel (undercoat) felts better than the tog (outer coat)

Romney wool (medium-coarse) – Has the potential to be very soft

Shetland wool (medium-coarse) – May include coarse hairs that are resistant to felting

Corriedale wool (medium-coarse) – Great for both wet felting and needle felting

Blue Faced Liecester wool (fine-medium) – Better for wet felting

Norwegian wool (medium-coarse) – Better for needle felting, more coarse than Merino and Corriedale

Needle Felting Foam

A needle felting pad or foam is used to help keep your creation grounded while working on it. It also protects surfaces (and your fingers!) from needle damage. Some felters prefer to use coarse brush. A thick, dense piece of foam works best. You don't necessarily need to purchase one as you can use alternatives that are found around your house. I actually use thick foam that was leftover packaging for a whiteboard I bought!

Other Supplies

As you become more experienced, you'll find other supplies and tools that fit your needs. However, finger protectors may be helpful or beginners who want to avoid stabbing their fingers while needle felting. Even if you are slow and careful, it is almost a guarantee that you'll poke yourself!

How to Needle Felt

Slowly pull the wool by gripping it further apart. Tear a piece that is at least 1/2 an inch thicker than the shape desired.

Roll to fibers into a ball. Do not use an excessive amount of wool. You want to layer and slowly add to your shape.

Start to poke the fibers with the needle, ensuring that you are stabbing in an up-and-down fashion being careful not to angle the needle. You should be pulling the needle out at the same angle you are inserting it into your piece.

Move the object around while poking with the needle to allow the fibers to felt evenly. Do not force the needle into any spots that feel firm. Move to a new area so that the shape firms uniformly.

Keep adding layers of wool until you reach the desired amount.

The fiber is felted once you see a smooth finish on the outside of your shape. There should not be an excessive amount of coarse fibers sticking out.

Needle Felting Projects

Needle Felted Gnome Tutorial – DIY Holiday Crafts

Grab a cuppa and mince pie and get creative with me, You can felt along with me or just watch and save for later. All you need is a handful of wool, any colours or type, and a felting needle. A cocktail stick will come in useful but it's not essential.

Skill level: Complete beginners – no crafting experience necessary

Time to make: Approximately 30 minutes

You will need:

15g any colour wool top/roving for the body

5g Wool top/roving or carded wool for the hat, in your choice of colour

Pinch of light colour for the nose

2g Wool top/roving, or curly wool for the beard, in your choice of colour

Enthusiasm

Nordic and Scandinavian style decor is so popular and I just love it. What I especially love are the charming Nordic gnomes. You may also see them referred to as Nisse, Tomte and Tonttu. Our house is full of them and they are super easy so here's a tutorial for you.

If you have never needle felted before or are an experienced felter this is a wonderful way to start and get you in the festive mood. It's simple and relaxing and so much fun to make.

This is just one style to get you started but there are so many variations that soon, like me, you will be tripping over them. So grab a cuppa, mince pie and some festive cheer and get creating.

1 – Hat: Make this first so the body fits the hat; much easier than trying to fit the hat to the body! You can go as small or tall as you like but this hat, when completed, is approx 20cm. The triangle template measurements are approx; base 10cm (slightly curved) and sides 12cm .

Layer your hat wool on your felting mat and pop your hat template on top of your wool, leaving a few extra centimetres of wool around each side. Top tip: Your wool shouldn't be too thick but make sure you can't see the felting mat through it

Make sure you can't see through the wool

2 – 'Draw' a line around the triangle with your needle to create a very rough outline

Draw' around the template

3 – Remove template and draw around the line a couple more times. This will be your fold line.

Make sure your line is visible

4 – Fold in the sides one at a time and start to felt to create a triangle; it will be a very rough shape to start with but you will tidy this up as the wool becomes more felted so stop fiddling with it!

Stop at the fold line

5 – Gently fold and felt each side until you have this rough shape; keep the excess at the top of your triangle because this is going to create your lovely pointy hat shape.

Repeat for all three sides

6 – Gently pull away from the base you are using, turn and repeat. Tip; any felting base will do (foam, rice bag etc), whatever your preference.

Keep turning regularly so it doesn't stick to the base

7 – Keep repeating the process until it starts to firm up.

Continue felting until it holds its shape

8 – Time to tidy up the shape; use your finger to fold in the sides that need straightening (doesn't have to be perfect). Be slow and careful so as not to stab your finger; you can use a finger guard but I find they just annoy me. However, I have lots of customers who get on with them just fine.

Be careful, the needle is sharp

9 – Your approx finished triangle which should be soft but firm and holds its shape.

Your finished hat shape; it doesn't have to be perfect

10 – Fold in half and felt along the side to mesh the fibres together. Keep turning and repeating until the hat is now firmly felted along the side so it doesn't pull apart when you gently pull it.

Fold in half and felt along the seam

11 – Open up the base of the hat and tidy up the line by folding in any rough edges and felting. Keep turning and felting until you are happy with the shape at the base of your Tomte hat

12 – Roll just the top 2/3 cm of your hat between the palm of your hands to firm up the top and point. This improves the look as well as allowing you to tip the point over to the side at a jaunty angle

Roll the tip in the palm of your hands to create a pointy hat

Use any colours you want for the hat

Basic Body Shape

Body shapes don't get much easier than this. Don't be too precious about needle marks and dimples because most of this will be covered by its big beard.

1 – Roll your wool (I have used natural white Shetland) into a basic barrel shape. It will do this automatically as you start to roll. Start with less than you need and build it up.

Most important! Do not start to felt with your needle until you have rolled at least half of it really tightly; trust me, this will save you a lot of felting time and applies to all body shapes made this way!

2 – Start stabbing all over with your needle (mind your fingers) as you continue to roll and remember to keep it tight. Tip: Check to see if your hat sits on top and if the body is too small add some more wool and felt again. If it's too big then continue to felt where the hat will sit to reduce the size.

3 – Continue to turn and felt until you have a more even and neater shape. You may end up with a narrower end which is fine because you will pop the hat onto this. Pay particular attention to the base which needs to be flat for stability. Tip; you can also press on the base once felted as the wool is pretty malleable.

4 – Flatten the base until it sits without wobbling.

5 – Pop on your hat and felt, gently, all around the edge until it is felted securely onto the body making sure the hat seam is at the back.

6 – Make the nose by rolling a pinch of white or flesh coloured wool in your hands just to rough it up. Place on your mat and continue to felt with your needle, turning all the time. Now place back into the palm of

your hands and roll vigorously until really firm and smooth.

Tip; you may have to do this a couple of times to get it right as it is very easy to add too much wool and have a huge nose if you have never needle felted before. Less is always more when it comes to needle felting.

7 – Place the nose on its side, just under the front of the hat and felt the end into the body.

9 – As you do this the nose will naturally rise into its correct position. Continue to felt around the base until it is firmly attached. The base of the hat should be sat just above the nose.

10 – Decide what type of beard you are going to have. I have used grey Jacob but

use whatever colour you wish. Curly locks also look really great.

11 – If using a straight wool pull off a small section and fold in half and start by felting it onto the body just under the nose. Don't worry about it being longer than the body because you will trim it to size (or not) once it is attached.

12 – Continue to felt along the fold and attach it up the side of the nose and along the hat line. Tip; you can push the wool under the hat line with your needle (don't bend it or you may break the needle) for a neater finish.

13 – Now trim your beard to your desired shape and style. I like mine quite 'raggy' so once I have got the length I then snip into the sides.

There you have it. One fabulous Tomte Christmas gnome! You can crease the hat or keep it straight. I like both. Told you it was easy!

Try different wool and add some fabulous locks for a different look. For the gnomes below I have used a lush teal batting with green silk fibres for the hat, and plant dyed, hand spun locks for the beard. The gnome on the right has a beard of grey Masham shot through with white silk.

But why would you stop there when the variations and colours are endless!

How To Needle Felt A Picture

I will be focusing on needle felting but you can adapt to suit whatever project you are working on.

Preparation and planning is really important. I find using a photograph of a landscape, animal, woodland scene etc for reference/inspiration really helpful. It can be the roughest of guides or very specific to the photograph or image you have in mind.

You may have a particular animal you want to incorporate into the picture which is also a great starting point; anything goes.

For this guide I am creating fields as the backdrop with a 2 D wooden gate, Herdwick Sheep and pebble wall in the foreground. It is called, 'Watching Me, Watching Ewe.' I know, cheese on toast right... but it was too good an opportunity not to. You should hear my pirate jokes. I save those for special occasions, usually workshops. #sorrynotsorry to anyone who has been at the receiving end of them...

Enough pre-amble, lets get started.

1 – Using a piece of *pre-felt for the back of your picture take a marker or chalk to, very roughly, draw out your idea on to the pre-felt: ZERO DRAWING SKILLS REQUIRED. This way you can ensure that you can fit in all the elements you want to use.

* I always use pure Shetland but any 100% wool felt is OK. Size of the pre-felt I used for this picture is approx 20cm square. A 30cm square is included in the picture pack.

2 – I am making a *Herdwick picture with a landscape backdrop and stone wall to get lots of 2D elements in there. It's quite a small picture; 20cm square to fit into some lovely shadow boxes I have. Also, starting with a smaller picture means there is less white space to fill which can be a little daunting and it takes less time.

3 – Mark your colours and objects so you know where your wool and 2D elements are going to sit. Keep it as simple as possible and remember these are just your guide lines.

4 – Time to get out your wool and needles. I am using a star 36/38 needles (good all rounders) and a punch tool (7 needles) to speed up the process.

5 – I felted the landscape first but you can start wherever you want depending on your picture style. I will be felting on my 2D

elements later and adding embellishment. Lay your colour on, or between the lines, you have drawn, and use your needle to gently felt into place. It doesn't have to be firmly felted but should stay in position.

I have used a mix of coarse wool tops and some semi carded wool tops that I had a lot of.

6 – Continue to gently needle felt your selected colours until the back ground is full.

7 – If you are happy with the layout then go ahead and felt the whole background more firmly (but not too flat), peeling it off your mat at intervals so it doesn't stick.

Don't worry if you have covered up some of your lines; remember they were just a guide.

You can also blend colours either by hand or using blending brushes (glorified dog brushes). For this picture I used a blend of Shetland blue top, light blue silk fibre and light grey Swaledale top for the sky.

8 – I wanted a distinct line separating the fields and used very thin strips of dark brown Jacob wool top to achieve this. Felt the lines quite firmly into the pre-felt which will push it down and give a little more depth.

Time to create some 2D elements.

9 – Wall

I have used lots of muted colours to create the pebbled wall appearance. Avoid all 'flat' colours by blending different colour wool by hand; if using the landscape box some colours will not need blending as they will already have texture and different shades. A soft palette works really well for this style of picture e.g purple blended with white, dark grey blended with white or light grey

Make your stones by rolling your wool into a very rough ball shape (this is not the shape you will end up with but will create dimension) and felting all over with your needle. Keep the wool moving as it firms up and don't try to make it even; have you ever seen even shapes on a dry stone wall... Make quite a few different shapes and sizes; mine are approx 1.5cm to 2.5cm then place them on your picture in the walled area to see how many more you will actually need.

Once done stitch or glue them into position; I'm not a purist and whichever you choose is fine. Clearly, using glue is so much faster and a strong fabric glue will do just fine as long as you give it a little time to dry. Using glue also allows you to move your pebbles about before the glue dries; you will be ready for a cuppa at this stage anyway.

10 – Time to make the Herdwick sheep head (or whichever animal you have chosen).

: How to needle felt a head shape You will want to flatten the back of the head so it sits nicely on your picture. You can then needle felt your eyes or use beads (included in the picture pack).

11- Start with a small length of white wool (approx 2g) and roll into a rough oval shape felting (stabbing gently with your needle) and tucking in the ends as you go. Gently felt until it holds its shape and turning as you felt. Continue to felt until you have achieved a rough egg/oval shape. Now flatten the back of the head by needle felting until it sits flat on the picture but don't attach it yet; it's ears are missing.

12 – Ears: For the ears take a pinch of white wool. Lay it on your pad and draw a rough circle with your felting needle and fold the wool around the line you have drawn, felting it into the centre. Turn over (to prevent from sticking) and repeat a few times, leaving one end loose (to attach to the head) and felt until flat, smooth and slightly firm. Repeat for other ear. Attach the loose end of each ear to the side of the head and felt or sew into position so it is peeping over the wall.

13 – Gently felt on very thin wisps (even thinner than that) onto the face to create the nose and mouth. N.B. Easiest way is to roll very thin wisps of wool between your fingers before felting to the face. Alternatively, you can sew on using black or dark grey thread.

14 – Add your gate by rolling and felting your brown wool into short lengths and overlapping for effect before gently felting into position. You may reposition a few times before you are happy with it.

15 – Add your wool for the body of your animal but don't felt it flat and keep it quite loose as this will create dimension. I have used loose curly grey locks.

16- Now add your foreground details. I have used greens and some locks for a grassy feel but be as creative as you wish. You could add flowers, butterflies, bees etc.

17 - Finishing touches make all the difference and as you can see I have used french knots (easy and absolutely no need to be perfect). . Curly locks also add more interest and dimension.

There you have it. Super easy 2D picture tutorial

HOW TO MAKE A WOOL NEEDLE FELTING MAT USING YOUR WASHING MACHINE

Yep, you read that right.

Yesterday I discovered that it is actually possible to SUCCESSFULLY create felt in your washing machine.

I've tried doing this on and off for years (because I find wet-felting by hand a bit of a faff) and the results have always been a bit disappointing.

The wool tops gather in clumps in all the wrong places and just look generally lumpy and rubbish.

But finally, after much trial and error I've stumbled across something which is a bit of a game changer.

As mentioned in my 'which needle felting pad should I use?' post I've been through a lot of different kinds, trying to find which is the best all-rounder.

I think I've found it – the 100% wool pad – and it's pretty easy to make on your own.

It's basically just a thick piece of wet felting (that's then been tidied up slightly) so it's not quite as rustic-looking.

One question I was asking when I first heard about these types of pads was – 'but if you're felting on to felt won't your needle felting work just get stuck to the pad?'

A couple of factors come into play here:

You shouldn't be leaving your work in the same position for long. If you're constantly turning and adjusting it as you stab, it won't get stuck.

The fibres in the wet felted piece are more tightly felted together, creating a much denser material. You'd have to really be trying to attach your work to the pad if it got stuck!

So on to the making.

What do we need? Luckily, things that you should have lying around the house if you're already a needle felter.

YOU WILL NEED:

Wool Roving

I've found that natural coloured wools are the best for this by far.

It seems like the coarser the wool the more readily it'll felt in the washing machine. The coloured merino I have is slightly less predictable.

The wool above is lovely grey Jacob wool. I didn't record how much I used exactly but you'll notice as we go that you need a fair bit.

To be honest – you can probably just use the wool that you've got the most of, but throw in some natural coloured wool if you have it.

Next up...

A big bit of material

Above is a bit of cotton calico I had lying around.

This is what your wool is going to go in when it goes into the washing machine.

Size-wise, this piece of fabric needs to be at least eight times as big as you want your finished felting mat to be. What you put in the machine will shrink A LOT.

As well as those two essential parts, you'll need the following...

A washing machine

Your normal laundry soap

Sewing machine (non-essential)

A needle and thread

Iron/ironing board

Scissors

And if you want your felting mat to look nice and tidy at the end:

Embroidery thread

Piece of felt a couple of inches bigger than your needle felting pad

PVA glue

And that's it.

So let's get started!

Open up your piece of material, imagining it's a book. On the right 'page', start placing strips of wool to form the first 'line'.

Keep creating rows of wool until the page is full. You now have your first layer of wool tops.

Now we need do another layer on top going from top to bottom instead of across.

Repeat, doing alternate left-right/top-bottom rows until you have FIVE layers of wool.

Your creation should look pretty bulky at this point. When you press your hand right down on to the fluffy mountain of wool you should be able to feel how thick the wool will be once it has felted. Since we're going to be folding it at the end you should feel that it's half the depth your pad is going to be. If it's not, add more layers until you're satisfied that it's thick enough.

When that's done, fold over the empty side of the material – closing 'the book'.

Now take your needle and thread and sew big, loose stitches around the open edges of the fabric. We're just tacking it in place so that wool doesn't fall out. I wouldn't recommend using a sewing machine at this point as it might move our wool around too much, and we want it to stay in position.

After that's done, carefully take your big woolly book over to the ironing board and using a cotton/linen setting press down on the material. This doesn't really help the felting process – we're just trying to flatten it a bit so that the next step is slightly easier!

By the time you've finished pressing it with the iron it should be roughly half the depth of when you started.

Once it's been flattened slightly take it over to your sewing machine and change the setting to the longest, loosest stitch that you can. I set my machine to 5mm stitch length with a tension of 1. Now stitch lines down through your felting about 10cm apart.

We want these stitches to hold the wool tops in place when they go into the washing machine, but we also want to be able to get them out easily when we retrieve our wool from the washing machine – that's why they mustn't be too tight. (Feel free to do a loose backstitch by hand if you don't have a sewing machine.)

Now it's time for the fun but slightly scary bit – putting your wool into the washing machine! I set my machine to a 40 degrees celsius wash (100 Fahrenheit) which lasted about 40 mins. I put a towel in too but I don't know if this made any difference. It certainly didn't harm anything, so if you have some washing to do anyway maybe put a few bits in with it.

Put your feet up and have a cuppa whilst you wait for the washing machine to do all the hard work!

Moment of truth time...when the washing machine has finished its cycle, take out your felt

Now rip the material open or unpick the stitches if you have to, to reveal our woolly creation.

It looks a bit weird at this point, but we can sort that out.

Iron the bobbly felt using the same settings as before and then take your scissors and trim the edges slightly to create a nice tidy shape. It might be closer to a rectangle shape, so trim it to a rectangle if that's the case – we want to waste as little as possible

This is where the sewing machine comes in again – set your sewing machine back to its normal settings (I do 1.4mm stitch length with tension set to 3) and stitch a straight line down each of the short edges.

Flip it over and you should now have something that's perfectly good to use as a felting pad. If you don't really care what it looks like as long as it's functional then you could stop here! However – I wanted to tidy it up as the underside and slightly scruffy edges made me a bit twitchy and less inclined to use it! So if you're the same as me, carry on reading...

Take your piece of felt and lay your own felt creation on top of it. You should have about an inch beyond each of the sides. (Ignore the extra bit I left to the right.)

Put a line of glue down one of the edges and stick it to the felt. Now do the same with the other edges and trim the corners.

Now that the thin felt is stuck in place we can tidy it up a bit but doing a neat stitch around the edge – I chose blanket stitch, but seeing as the edges of felt don't fray you could do a small running stitch or backstitch.

Tadaaaaa! And there you have your very own wool felt mat.

Materials•

1 piece of bubble wrap (about 20" × 20"), with small bubbles •

Felting net or fly screen from hardware store (same dimensions as piece of bubble wrap)

•Bar of soap (A low-suds soap, such as an olive-oil based one, is easier to work with because it produces fewer suds.)

•4-8 ounces of Merino-type wool roving tops (mixed colors); Corriadale wool is also a good felting fiber.

•A plastic bag

•Warm water•

Sponge•Small bowl

•Old bath towelnote: When you have finished felting, your piece will have shrunk to about half of the size of the bubble wrap piece you started with.

Directions

1. Lay the towel on your work surface.

2. Place the bubble wrap on top of the towel, bubble side up.

3. Choose one of your Merino-type f ibers and hold it in one hand, about 5" to 8" from one end. 4. With your other hand, gently pull some fibers loose from the wool roving (or tops) and lay them on the bubble wrap, starting 3" to 4" from the edges. It is important to leave Bits of silk tops can add

sheen and a silky texture to your felted piece. this space between the edge of the bubble wrap and the fibers.

5. Repeat the process, laying out the f ibers and overlapping them slightly, much as tiles are laid on a roof. All these fibers should be aligned in the same direction.

6. Lay out a second layer of fibers on top of the first, but at right angles to the first layer. This layer could be the same color as the first layer, or you may choose a different color. You now have 2 layers: one running north-south, and the other east-west.

7. Now take some fine strands of wool roving in other colors and lay them randomly across your piece. At this stage you can also add thread snippets, silk fibers, and so on, to create an elaborate surface on your felt. You can be as creative as you like.

8. Lay the felting net over the piece.

9. Use your sponge to wet down the f ibers through the net with hot water to the the touch (not scalding). Two applications of water with your sponge should be enough,

but be prepared to add more if required. It is essential that all of the fibers are wet.

10. Lightly rub the bar of soap across the surface of the net, and then gently stroke the net with your hands. This will start to work the soap into the fibers. Use a plastic bag over your hands for this step to protect your hands and help to minimize pilling.

11. As soon as the fibers appear to "pill" through the net, remove the net and continue to rub the fibers gently by hand for about one minute or so.

12. If you would like a more defined edge to your felt, fold the bubble wrap over so that the irregular edges of the fibers are folded back onto the piece.

13. Now roll up the bubble wrap with your piece still inside it, forming a tube. Keeping the "tube" intact, gently roll the tube back and forth to continue the felting process.

14. Unroll the tube, turn the bubble wrap and piece 90 degrees, and roll it up in the new direction. Gently roll the tube back and forth to continue the felting process. The

piece has now been rolled both top-to-bottom and side-to-side. It is important to rotate the felt because it shrinks in the direction that you are rolling it. By now you will have a piece of felt in the "pre-felt" stage. Note that several things have occurred

: •The fibers have started to mesh together

. •Colored fibers laid on top have started to migrate through to the bottom, and the fibers from the first layer have moved towards the top.

•The piece has shrunk as you have felted it.

15. Repeat step 14 several times until your felted fabric has shrunk to about one half of its original size, or it is sufficiently felted for your needs. Rinse in warm water, then gently squeeze out the excess water.

Allow your piece to dry. note: You can adjust the size and shape of the felt while it is wet by either continuing to roll it to shorten it, or by carefully stretching it if it has shrunk too much. These last steps are part of the hardening or milling process.

Traditional methods involve fiercely rolling the wool fibers in hand-woven reed mats or "mother felts" so that the fibers shrink and mesh together to produce a durable, robust fabric. I prefer to have a soft felt to work with, one which is not fully "hardened." When felt is destined for further embellishment for decorative purposes such as wall hangings, pictures, adornments, it obviously doesn't need to be as strong as the felt used by the nomads for clothing and shelter. Don't be afraid to experiment.

The experience you have in making your felt will give you the confidence to make this process your own. If you would like to further embellish your felt with beads, stitching, and mixed media, watch for my second article in the next issue of Cloth Paper Scissors.

Fiber effects colorful needle-felted trading cards big fluffy bundles of carded wool, lamb-soft tails of curling top, and silky strands of intense hue beckon spinners and knitters.

Who can resist dye-batch names like "lollipop," "hot peppers," and "moon goddess"? If owning sheep is not your cup of tea, there is undoubtedly someone in your community who thrives on it. My semi-rural town is rich with familyowned operations producing a delicious artist's paint box of handdyed, unspun fibers.

But what if you're not gifted with the tools to turn roving into yarn?

You can still join in the fun by learning the inexpensive art of needle felting. With a variety of fibers, you can create a painterly effect. Subtle differences in color allow shadows and highlights, just as if you were creating with watercolors. If you're truly ambitious, you can purchase plain wool or silk roving and dye it yourself. Be sure to use dyes appropriate for animal material, such as acid dyes.

Each type of material requires a different dye process in order to create rich color and washable results. There are even new plant-based alternatives to wool and silk, like soy silk and hemp, as well as sustainable green fibers made from bamboo and other materials.

Materials

- Ruler

- Scissors

- Felt pieces

- Felting needle

- Foam felting block

- Roving (assorted wool, silk, soy)

- Fabric pieces

- Fusible webbing

- Iron optional

- Embroidery floss

- Beads

- Sewing machine and thread

- Oil pastels

This simple artist trading card (ATC) project is a great introduction to the craft and a good excuse to indulge in some ultra-soft roving.

Preparation

1. Choose a felt color for the background of your artist trading card. Both wool and synthetic felt work nicely for this project, so choose whichever gives you the feeling you want.

2. Cut backgrounds slightly larger than ATC size (2½" × 3½"), as the surface will shrink a bit as you felt. It's better to start larger and trim when you are done than to end up with an undersized card.

3. To speed up the process, you can cut a template out of cardstock and zip around it with a rotary cutter. I keep a bunch of pre-cut felt bases with my supplies, so I can start a new one without missing a beat.

4. Gather some fibers for your project. Any loose fibers will do; I combine natural and synthetic fibers on my ATCs. You will see wool spinning f ibers referred to as roving, top, or sliver (pronounced with a long "i"). These should form the base of your image because their fibers will more easily become entangled with the base felt, creating that familiar felted look. But throw in some other fibers for fun, like tussah, silk hankies, or throwster's waste. You can mix them up with the wool or use them on top for an added splash of color

. 5. Determine what kind of image you want to create on the front of your card. Start with larger, less complex shapes and work towards more intricate designs as you gain experience. A simple heart or flower is a nice beginning.

Needle-felting basics Here's a quick introduction to needle felting

.   It's much less intimidating than traditional soap and water felting; the first time I saw a demo, I was entranced. It's so easy that it feels almost silly. But the results are beautiful and look very much like traditionally felted designs.

You'll need a special felting needle, but they're very inexpensive. They are usually shaped like an "L" with an extremely sharp point on the long side. Notches are cut along the shaft and the resulting barbs cause the fibers to get trapped on the back side of the base felt.

There are other types of felting devices available, with four, six, or more needles attached, or you may have seen the popular electric needle-felting machines, which look like sewing machines and make needle felting a breeze. note: Hand felting needles come in various gauges and each will be suitable for a different type of roving or project.

Try several to determine which you prefer.

A middle-of-the-road 36- or 38-gauge is useful for most things. The only other equipment you need is a piece of thick foam for felting into. You can find it with the other felting supplies, or improvise, but make sure the foam is thick enough to prevent the needle from reaching the bottom (and a body part!).Felting

1. Place a pre-cut felt base on the felting foam.

2. Pull a small tuft of roving and fold or roll it into a loose ball roughly the size of the image you want to create. Lay it on the felt and poke the needle into it a few times to secure it to the foam.

3. From that point, poke the needle into the roving repeatedly until it begins to form a bond with the base. Be extra careful to know where your fingers are in relation to the needle at all times. After poking for awhile, pick the base up from the foam and move it to another position. You'll see that the roving has migrated to the back of the felt base. note: It is only necessary to push the needle into the foam 1/2" or less.

4. Continue poking the roving, tucking and folding the edges over with the needle as

you go to form the image you are trying to create.

5. Once you've outlined the basic form, select small tufts of different colors and place them on top of the already felted area, then felt over them again to meld them into the picture. You can create highlights and shading with various shades of wool or silk. Go ahead and mix different kinds of roving and even lengths of fun fibers and yarns. Many things will felt up nicely.

6. Add embroidery stitches, machine stitching, or beads to finish your project. You can also add more highlights or shading with oil pastels, but use a gentle hand so that you don't tug at the fibers.

7. Once you've finished the front, stretch the ATC with your fingers to make sure it's flat and not bunched up. Measure and trim it to the correct size, 2½" × 3½".

8. Cut a piece of backing fabric the same size and iron it to the back of the ATC, using fusible web

. 9. Create a blanket stitch border with floss or fancy machine stitches.

Conclusion

Needle felting is an incredibly easy craft to get into as it only requires some wool, a special needle, and maybe even some foam. This hobby is best for those who love fiber arts or making miniatures. You can be as simple or as detailed as you'd like in your creations.

By just repeatedly poking the needle into the wool, the fibers start to become denser allowing you to form a variety of shapes. The best needle to use for beginners would be a 38-gauge spiral or triangular needle with numerous notches but can vary based on your personal preference. There are tons of different options for wool, but felters tend to lean towards medium-coarse fibers as it is easier to manipulate while still leaving a relatively smooth finish. Lastly,

make sure you do your work on a thick piece
of dense form to make things easier.